FREEDOM'S PROMISE

JOHN LEWIS

CIVIL RIGHTS LEADER AND CONGRESSMAN

BY DUCHESS HARRIS, JD, PHD

WITH TAMMY GAGNE

Core Library

An Imprint of Abdo Publishing
abdobooks.com

Cover image: As a politician and an activist, John Lewis
has spent his life fighting for civil rights.

abdobooks.com

Published by Abdo Publishing, a division of ABDO, PO Box 398166,
Minneapolis, Minnesota 55439. Copyright © 2020 by Abdo Consulting
Group, Inc. International copyrights reserved in all countries. No part of this
book may be reproduced in any form without written permission from the
publisher. Core Library™ is a trademark and logo of Abdo Publishing.

Printed in the United States of America, North Mankato, Minnesota
092019
012020

Cover Photo: Jim Lo Scalzo/EPA-EFE/Shutterstock Images
Interior Photos: Jim Lo Scalzo/EPA-EFE/Shutterstock Images, 1; Bill Clark/CQ Roll Call/AP
Images, 5; Bettmann/Getty Images, 6–7, 21, 24–25; Everett Collection/Newscom, 9, 29; AP
Images, 10; Rainer Lesniewski/Shutterstock Images, 13; Marion Post Wolcott/Everett Collection/
Newscom, 16–17; Rudolph Faircloth/AP Images, 18; Red Line Editorial, 27; Jessica McGowan/
Getty Images News/Getty Images, 31; J. Scott Applewhite/AP Images, 34–35, 43; Carolyn Kaster/
AP Images, 39

Editor: Maddie Spalding
Series Designer: Ryan Gale

Library of Congress Control Number: 2019942101

Publisher's Cataloging-in-Publication Data

Names: Harris, Duchess, author. | Gagne, Tammy, author.
Title: John Lewis: civil rights leader and congressman / by Duchess Harris and Tammy Gagne
Other title: civil rights leader and congressman
Description: Minneapolis, Minnesota : Abdo Publishing, 2020 | Series: Freedom's promise |
    Includes online resources and index.
Identifiers: ISBN 9781532190858 (lib. bdg.) | ISBN 9781532176708 (ebook)
Subjects: LCSH: Lewis, John, 1940 February 21---Juvenile literature. | Civil rights workers--
    United States--Biography--Juvenile literature. | Legislators--United States--
    Biography--Juvenile literature. | African Americans--Civil rights--Southern
    States--Juvenile literature. | Great March on Washington (1963 : Washington,
    D.C.)--Juvenile literature. | African American legislators--Biography--Juvenile
    literature.
Classification: DDC 323.09 [B]--dc23

CONTENTS

A LETTER FROM DUCHESS

John Lewis's parents were sharecroppers who rented a small house in Alabama. They were eventually able to get their own land. They were proud of their son John when he became the first person in the family to go to college. John's parents thought he would become a preacher. He was known to gather the chickens in the yard so he could practice giving sermons.

Once John left home, his life changed. At age 18 he met Martin Luther King Jr. His parents were worried about his involvement in the civil rights movement, but John kept working. His courage helped make it possible for his parents to vote.

This book is about a man who has fought for what he believes in for more than 50 years. When he spoke at the 1963 March on Washington, he was considered a young radical. Now he is seen as an elder statesman. He shows how leadership develops over time. Please join me on a journey to learn about a man who fought for social justice and freedom alongside King and still fights today.

Duchess Harris

John Lewis walks up the steps of the US Capitol.

BLOODY SUNDAY

I t was Sunday, March 7, 1965. The day began with a great deal of hope. John Lewis and approximately 600 other activists set out on a journey that morning. They left the Brown Chapel African Methodist Episcopal Church in Selma, Alabama. They silently walked two by two down the city streets. The group planned to march all the way to Montgomery. The capital city was 50 miles (80 km) away. They were staging a peaceful protest for equal rights, including voting rights.

The Fifteenth Amendment to the US Constitution gave African American men the right to vote in 1870. Fifty years later, the

Lewis, *right*, and other civil rights protesters marched across the Edmund Pettus Bridge in Selma in 1965.

Nineteenth Amendment passed. It gave all women the right to vote. But many white people in the South tried to stop Black people from voting. In 1965 approximately 15,000 African Americans in Selma were eligible to vote. But only 300 of them had managed to register. In Selma and many other parts of the South, African Americans had to take literacy tests to register. Officials sometimes gave these tests to white people too. But the tests given to Black people were more difficult. Officials did not want Black people to pass these tests.

The 1960s was the height of the American civil rights movement. Lewis and other civil rights activists fought racial discrimination. The protesters in Selma were marching to the state capital to register more Black voters. The march was also a protest against police violence. Police often targeted and attacked Black people. On February 18, 1965, a state trooper had shot and killed a Black man named Jimmie Lee Jackson near Selma. Black activists called for an end to this violence.

African Americans line up outside a courthouse in 1946 in Atlanta, Georgia, to try to register to vote.

Lewis and the other protesters did not get very far. After walking six blocks, they encountered approximately 150 state troopers and police officers. The protesters were trying to cross the Edmund Pettus Bridge. The police ordered them to turn back. Lewis had told the activists to remain calm if police tried to stop them. They did exactly as he said. Many of the marchers simply sat down.

The police responded with violence. They used clubs and whips to beat many of the protesters. They also released tear gas. Officers riding on horseback trampled some of the activists. Many activists were injured. A local hospital treated 58 protesters,

including Lewis. He suffered a skull fracture after state troopers beat him. Lewis thought he was going to die. A day that had begun with so much hope would be referred to in history books as Bloody Sunday.

NOT YET OVER

News agencies informed the nation about what had happened in Selma. Viewers were outraged by the violence. In response, people organized protests. Demonstrations took place in more than 80 US cities over the next two days. People took to the streets. They carried banners that read "We march with Selma!"

Civil rights leader Martin Luther King Jr. urged his supporters to travel to Selma. He wanted them to help him finish the march Lewis and the others had begun. This was not an easy task. The protest was stopped again when President Lyndon B. Johnson called it off. He asked King to wait until later in the month. Johnson needed time to arrange for protection for

Photographers captured the violence on Bloody Sunday, including the state troopers' attack on Lewis.

PERSPECTIVES

MARTIN LUTHER KING JR.

Martin Luther King Jr. appeared on the NBC news program *Meet the Press* in 1965. It was just three days after Bloody Sunday. Journalist Ned Brooks was the show's host. Brooks told King that former president Harry Truman had called the march "silly." Truman had also said that all the march did was attract attention. King told NBC's viewers that the march was not silly at all. He said that it showed how Black people were mistreated. He called the attempted march the most effective civil rights protest in the South.

the marchers. He did not want anyone else to get hurt.

Johnson supported the activists. He gave a speech before the US Congress on March 15. He urged Congress members to pass a voting rights bill. This bill later passed into law as the Voting Rights Act of 1965. Johnson also kept his promise to help the protesters finish their march. He ordered the US Army to join the Alabama National Guard in protecting the protesters.

THE SELMA
MARCH

Protesters began the Selma March for the third time on March 21, 1965. So many people showed up that parts of Highway 80 had to be shut down. This map shows the route the marchers took (the green line). Does this map help you better understand the march? Why or why not?

THE VOTING RIGHTS ACT

Beginning in the 1870s, states created obstacles that kept Black people from voting. These obstacles included poll taxes and literacy tests. Poll taxes were fees people had to pay when registering to vote. Most Black people could not afford these taxes. There were few job opportunities for Black people. They were often stuck in low-paying jobs. Many African Americans also struggled to pass the literacy tests. Voting officials often made the test harder for Black people than for white people. For example, they often asked Black people difficult questions about US laws or the federal government. The Voting Rights Act of 1965 outlawed these obstacles.

On March 21, a second wave of protesters gathered in Selma. Some had marched in the previous attempts. Others joined the protest for the first time.

The group began where the first march had ended on Bloody Sunday. King led approximately 8,000 marchers across the Edmund Pettus Bridge. More people joined the march along the way. Lewis participated. By the time the group reached Montgomery, it had grown to approximately 25,000 people. They reached the capital on March 25.

Completing the Selma March was a big step for the civil rights movement. But it was far from the end of the fight for equality. Lewis made it his life's work to keep standing up for civil rights. By the early 1960s, he had become a prominent leader in the civil rights movement. He later made equality a top priority as a politician.

EXPLORE ONLINE

Chapter One discusses the 1965 Selma March. The article below talks about the fiftieth anniversary of this event. How is the information from the website the same as the information in Chapter One? What new information did you learn?

FIFTY YEARS AFTER BLOODY SUNDAY
abdocorelibrary.com/john-lewis

SITTING IN AND SPEAKING OUT

John Lewis was born on February 21, 1940, near Troy, Alabama. His parents were Eddie and Willie Mae Lewis. They made their living as sharecroppers. Sharecroppers farmed land that belonged to someone else. They gave part of each harvest to the landowner as rent. Sharecroppers did not make much money. But there were few job options for Black people in the South. As a result, many African Americans became sharecroppers.

John spent his youth in segregated schools. Segregation is the separation of

In the early 1900s, most Black farmers were sharecroppers.

In segregated schools, the supplies and resources given to Black children were often of lower quality than those given to white children.

people into groups. In the South, Jim Crow laws enforced segregation. Black children could not attend the same schools as white children. Black people were set apart from white people in many other ways too. For example, Black people could not use the same drinking fountains as white people.

John thought segregation was wrong. But his parents discouraged him from speaking out about it. They knew this would anger white people. They worried that fighting segregation would put their son in danger.

Still, John could not ignore the injustices he and other African Americans faced. His interest in changing the way Black people were treated continued into his teen years. He wanted to attend Troy State College after high school. It was a whites-only school. He sent in an application, but the school would not accept him. John's parents convinced him to apply to a school that accepted Black students. John enrolled at the American Baptist Theological Institute and later at Fisk University. Both schools were in Nashville, Tennessee.

John attended college in the late 1950s and 1960s. While in college, he learned about peaceful protests. He participated in sit-ins. During a sit-in, Black people went to a segregated place and calmly sat down. They refused to leave. This was a protest against segregation. Many sit-ins happened at lunch counters. Lunch counters were popular hangouts in the 1960s. These were small restaurants where customers sat on one side of a long table. Lunch counters were often segregated. Black customers had to sit apart from white customers. Many establishments would not even serve Black customers.

DANGEROUS TIMES

Participating in protests often came with a cost. Not all demonstrations remained peaceful. Sometimes white people and even police officers became violent. They attacked Black protesters.

In 1961 Lewis took part in the Freedom Rides. These were protests against segregated bus terminals. Passengers spent time at these facilities as they waited for buses to arrive or depart. Bus terminals in the South had separate waiting areas for Black people.

Lewis was part of the original group of Freedom Riders.

ROSA PARKS

One of Lewis's role models was Rosa Parks. Parks became well known in 1955 after she refused to give her seat on a bus to a white man. When Lewis was young, everyone told him not to fight segregation. They said he should not get in the way. But Parks inspired Lewis and many other people to take action.

Freedom Riders Lewis, *left*, and James Zwerg, *right*, were injured when a mob attacked them at a Montgomery bus stop on May 20, 1961.

The group was made up of seven African Americans and six white people. The Congress of Racial Equality (CORE) organized the Freedom Rides. CORE is a civil rights organization. The first Freedom Ride happened on May 4, 1961. Lewis was still a college student at this time. Lewis and the other Freedom Riders boarded a bus in Washington, DC. It was headed to New Orleans, Louisiana. The bus stopped in Rock Hill, South Carolina, on May 12. Lewis and two other Freedom Riders headed toward the whites-only waiting area. Lewis did not even make it through the door. Two white men stopped him. They kicked him and punched him in

FLOYD MANN

Floyd Mann was Alabama's safety commissioner in the early 1960s. The safety commissioner is the head of the police. Mann was present when violence broke out at a bus stop in Montgomery in 1961. Lewis and other activists were taking part in a Freedom Ride. Mann was in favor of segregation. But he wanted to stop the violence. He kept a white man from hitting Lewis on the head with a baseball bat. Mann pointed his gun at the man. He ordered the man to put down his weapon. In 1989 Lewis met Mann at a dedication for a civil rights memorial in Montgomery. Lewis told him, "You saved my life." Mann responded, "I'm right proud of your career."

the face. They attacked the other two Freedom Riders too. Still, Lewis did not let this attack stop him from speaking out. He kept protesting at bus terminals. He was knocked unconscious at some of these demonstrations.

Soon more civil rights activists noticed Lewis. They saw that he was a natural leader. In 1963 the Student Nonviolent Coordinating Committee (SNCC) elected him as its chair. Lewis had helped create this civil rights group. He served as the chair of SNCC (often pronounced "snik") for the next three years.

Through SNCC, Lewis planned student sit-ins and other demonstrations. He was arrested more than 40 times. He was seriously injured at many of these events. Still, he never fought back against his attackers. He supported peaceful protests.

FURTHER EVIDENCE

Chapter Two discusses Lewis's involvement in the Freedom Rides. What was one of the chapter's main points? What evidence was given to support that point? The website below describes the activists who took part in the Freedom Rides. Does the information on the website support the point you identified? Does it present new evidence?

MEET THE PLAYERS: FREEDOM RIDERS
abdocorelibrary.com/john-lewis

BECOMING A LEADER

On August 28, 1963, Lewis participated in a civil rights march in Washington, DC. Approximately 250,000 activists gathered in front of the Lincoln Memorial. King led the march. The activists walked to the Washington Monument. This protest was called the March on Washington for Jobs and Freedom. Black and white people alike took part in the march. They called for equal rights and an end to discrimination. They hoped to inspire more people to stand up for civil rights.

Lewis was one of six activists who helped organize the march. The other activists were

Lewis gave an inspiring speech near the Lincoln Memorial at the 1963 March on Washington.

King, A. Philip Randolph, Whitney Young, James Farmer, and Roy Wilkins. Together, they were known as the Big Six. They were among the most prominent civil rights leaders in the country. Lewis was by far the youngest in this group. He was just 23 years old. He had graduated from the American Baptist Theological Institute in 1961. He was continuing his education at Fisk University. He studied religion and philosophy.

Lewis gave a speech at the March on Washington. In it, he said that the time for patience had passed. He urged people across the country to stand up for civil rights. He spoke of the importance of demanding freedom and voting rights.

MAKING A DIFFERENCE

In 1964 Lewis helped lead a voter registration drive. He encouraged activists to help Black people register to vote in Mississippi. This voter registration drive was called Freedom Summer.

THE BIG SIX

NAME	CIVIL RIGHTS WORK
James Farmer (1920–1999)	Founded CORE
Martin Luther King Jr. (1929–1968)	Served as president of the Southern Christian Leadership Conference, a group that organized nonviolent protests
A. Philip Randolph (1889–1979)	Created one of the first labor unions for African Americans
Roy Wilkins (1901–1981)	Served as executive director of the National Association for the Advancement of Colored People, a civil rights group
Whitney Young (1921–1971)	Worked to end employment discrimination and headed the National Urban League, which fought for justice for African Americans

This chart shows the other Big Six activists and their contributions to the civil rights movement. How were their causes and efforts similar to Lewis's civil rights work?

On June 15, 1964, approximately 300 activists arrived in Mississippi as part of the Freedom Summer project. The next day, three of the activists went missing. Their bodies were found six weeks later. Two of the activists were white. One was African American. Ku Klux Klan (KKK) members had beaten them to death. The KKK was a white hate group. It did not want African Americans to gain equal rights. The KKK used violence to intimidate Black people. KKK members attacked and even killed African Americans.

By 1966 many SNCC members were frustrated because change was happening slowly. Some did not think peaceful protests were having much of an effect. They saw violence as the only way to get people's attention. They began to protest more aggressively. But Lewis still believed it was important to demonstrate peacefully. Some SNCC

Lewis, *third from left*, and other activists met with President Lyndon B. Johnson, *right*, in 1965 to discuss civil rights issues.

members still shared this belief. In 1966 they left the group along with Lewis.

In January 1967, Lewis met Lillian Miles. Miles was a librarian at Atlanta University. They married less than a year later. They bought a house in Atlanta, Georgia. They later adopted a son. They named him John-Miles Lewis.

Lewis graduated from Fisk University in 1967. He stayed dedicated to civil rights. Less than a year later, Lewis and the rest of the civil rights community faced a devastating loss. Lewis learned that King had been killed in Memphis, Tennessee. Lewis had lost a dear friend. And the country had lost an important civil rights leader.

ENTRY INTO POLITICS

In Atlanta, Lewis headed the Voter Education Project (VEP). This organization helped raise money for civil rights groups. The VEP assisted in voter registration efforts. It kept track of voter registration in Black communities. It also studied elections in the South and the roles that race was playing in them. The VEP studied data about gender and voting too.

In 1977 Lewis decided to run for public office. He campaigned for a spot in the US House of Representatives. He wanted to represent Georgia's Fifth District. But he lost the race.

Lewis supported Jimmy Carter's grandson, Jason Carter, *left*, when Jason ran for governor of Georgia in 2014.

Jimmy Carter was elected president of the United States in 1977. Lewis knew Carter. They had met when Carter was the governor of Georgia. They shared many political views. They were both Democrats. After Carter became president, he offered Lewis a job. He wanted Lewis to lead a federal agency called ACTION. This agency oversaw volunteer groups such as the Peace Corps. As the director of ACTION, Lewis was in charge of 250,000 volunteers.

In 1981 Lewis decided to try running for office at the local level. He won a seat on the Atlanta City Council. He spent much of his time on the council supporting local issues. He supported community programs that helped people create good relationships with their neighbors. He also fought for ethics in government. He believed politicians should always be up-front and honest.

In 1986 Lewis again campaigned to become a representative for Georgia's Fifth District. This time, he defeated his opponent. He continued to win elections, remaining in office for more than three decades.

BEATING THE ODDS

Lewis ran against Democrat Julian Bond for a seat in the House of Representatives in 1986. Bond was also African American. Both men had grown up in the South. They had both experienced discrimination and been active in the civil rights movement. But Bond had the support of many Black politicians in Georgia. Lewis did not. Many people underestimated him. But he was determined to win. Lewis's fellow Atlanta councilman Bill Campbell called him "the little engine that could."

STRAIGHT TO THE
SOURCE

President Barack Obama gave a speech at the Lincoln Memorial on the fiftieth anniversary of the March on Washington. He said,

> They [the marchers] had learned . . . that freedom is not given; it must be won through struggle and discipline, persistence and faith. . . .
>
> That was the spirit young people like John Lewis brought that day. That was the spirit that they carried with them like a torch back to their cities and their neighborhoods, that steady flame of conscience and courage that would sustain them. . . . Through setbacks and heartbreaks and gnawing doubt, that flame of justice flickered and never died.

Source: Washington Post Staff. "President Obama's Speech on the 50th Anniversary of the March on Washington." *Washington Post*. Washington Post, August 28, 2013. Web. Accessed June 28, 2019.

What's the Big Idea?
Take a close look at this passage. What connections did Obama make between John Lewis's work in the civil rights movement and freedom? What were the effects of the March on Washington?

STILL MAKING HISTORY

After Lewis was first elected to the House of Representatives, he quickly got to work. Since 1986, he has sponsored many bills that have become laws. Several of them relate to civil rights and African American history. One bill that he sponsored was the King Holiday and Service Act of 1994. This act made community service programs part of Martin Luther King Jr. Day. Martin Luther King Jr. Day is celebrated each year on January 20. It is a holiday that marks King's birthday. This date became a federal holiday in 1986. Lewis thought community

Lewis has a reputation as a powerful speaker and educator.

service was the most fitting way to honor King's life.

In 1998 Lewis published his memoir. It is called *Walking with the Wind: A Memoir of the Movement*. In the book, he explores his early life as a civil rights activist. Reviewers praised the book for being so different from other memoirs about the civil rights era. Other memoirs usually told stories about well-known civil rights leaders. Lewis's memoir shared new stories about largely unknown champions of civil rights.

Many Americans did not know about activists Diane Nash or Fannie Lou Hamer until they read his book.

In 2007 Lewis sponsored a bill called the Emmett Till Unsolved Civil Rights Crime Act. This bill was created to help solve civil rights crimes. Some murders and other hate crimes have gone unsolved since the 1950s. This bill was named after Emmett Till. Emmett was a 14-year-old Black boy who was murdered in Mississippi in 1955. A white woman claimed that he flirted with her. The woman's husband and another white man killed Emmett. They thought Black people should not flirt with white people. They saw this as an insult. An all-white jury found the men not guilty after the men denied killing Emmett. The woman later admitted that she had lied. Emmett had not flirted with her. The men later confessed to beating Emmett before shooting him in the head.

Lewis has also sponsored successful bills on other important issues. He has helped make homeownership more affordable. He has also helped people keep their health insurance and retirement benefits. He believes health care should be a right guaranteed to all Americans. Other bills that Lewis has sponsored have helped small businesses.

SHARING HIS STORIES

In 2012 Lewis published his second book. It was called *Across That Bridge: A Vision for Change and the Future of America*. It included stories from Lewis's past. Lewis also shared his thoughts on how everyone can make a difference.

Lewis has also written several graphic novels for young adults. Three of these books are part of

A HIGH HONOR

President Barack Obama awarded Lewis the Presidential Medal of Freedom in 2011. This award is given to people who make important contributions to the nation. At the ceremony, Obama spoke about Lewis's experience on Bloody Sunday. He said that Lewis "faced down death so that all of us could share equally in the joys of life."

In 2011 President Barack Obama awarded Lewis the Presidential Medal of Freedom.

the March trilogy. This trilogy tells the story of Lewis's

fight for civil rights. Lewis hopes these books will teach

new generations about the civil rights movement. The

final book in the series was released in 2016. It won

the National Book Award and the Coretta Scott King Book Award.

After the March trilogy, Lewis began writing a graphic novel called *Run: Book One*. It continues the story of Lewis's activism. It begins just after the Voter Rights Act passed. Lewis hopes the book will inspire young people to get involved in politics. As the title suggests, this book will also be part of a series.

Lewis continues to organize and participate in peaceful protests. In 2016 he staged a sit-in on the House floor. The purpose of the sit-in was to protest Republican congress members' actions. The congress members were not allowing people to debate a gun control bill. A total of 170 Democratic congress members took part in the sit-in.

Lewis understands that true change takes time and patience. He has dedicated his life to inspiring change and fighting for people's rights. He continues to work to create a better future for all Americans.

STRAIGHT TO THE
SOURCE

Lewis urges young people to stand up for their beliefs. In *Across That Bridge: A Vision for Change and the Future of America*, he offered some advice. He wrote:

> Read history, study what happened in the past as you devise your plan. . . . Your opponent is not a single person, but the forces of violence, separation, and division. Recognize that people have the power to change. If people are convinced of the worthiness of your cause, soul-to-soul communication is the pathway to changing hearts and minds. Take action that demonstrates the dignity and humanity of your cause and you may find yourself the leader of an effective movement. That is the difference between a dream and a plan.

Source: John Lewis. *Across That Bridge: A Vision for Change and the Future of America*. New York: Hachette Books, 2012. Print. 145.

Consider Your Audience

Adapt this passage for a different audience, such as your friends. Write a blog post conveying this same information for the new audience. How does your post differ from the original text and why?

FAST FACTS

- John Lewis was born near Troy, Alabama, on February 21, 1940.

- As a college student, Lewis learned about peaceful protests. He believed nonviolent demonstrations were an effective way to bring about change.

- In 1963 Lewis was named the chairman of the Student Nonviolent Coordinating Committee (SNCC). This group helped plan civil rights protests.

- In 1965 he led the first attempt of the Selma March to register Black voters in Alabama. Police attacked him and fractured his skull.

- Lewis helped organize the 1963 March on Washington. He also gave a speech at the march.

- After graduating from college, Lewis moved to Georgia, where he headed the Voter Education Project.

- Lewis was elected to the House of Representatives in 1986. He has been reelected to the seat for more than three decades.

- Lewis has sponsored many bills that have passed into law. He has written two memoirs and several graphic novels about his involvement in the civil rights movement.

STOP AND
THINK

Surprise Me

This book discusses Lewis's work as a civil rights activist and politician. After reading this book, what two or three facts about his life did you find most surprising? Write a few sentences about each fact. Why did you find each fact surprising?

You Are There

Chapter Three talks about the 1963 March on Washington. Imagine that you took part in this march. Write a letter to a friend or family member about what the experience was like. What did you see and hear?

Take a Stand

This book discusses the Voting Rights Act of 1965 and how the Supreme Court ruled to limit it in 2013. Why are equal voting rights important? How do you think people's voting rights could be protected today?

GLOSSARY

campaign
to promote oneself for
a position

demonstration
a public protest to raise
awareness of an issue

discrimination
the unjust treatment of a
group of people based
on their race, gender, or
other characteristics

labor union
an organization of
workers that fights for
better employment rights
and benefits

philosophy
the study of people's ideas
and values

protester
a person who
demonstrates strong
opposition to something

segregation
the separation of
people based on race or
other factors

sponsor
to propose a bill

tear gas
a type of gas that causes
extreme eye irritation

ONLINE
RESOURCES

To learn more about John Lewis, visit our free resource websites below.

Visit **abdocorelibrary.com** or scan this QR code for free Common Core resources for teachers and students, including vetted activities, multimedia, and booklinks, for deeper subject comprehension.

Visit **abdobooklinks.com** or scan this QR code for free additional online weblinks for further learning. These links are routinely monitored and updated to provide the most current information available.

LEARN
MORE

Haskins, Jim, and Kathleen Benson. *The Story of Civil Rights Hero John Lewis*. New York: Lee & Low Books, 2018.

Lewis, John, and Andrew Aydin. *March: Book Two*. Marietta, GA: Top Shelf Productions, 2015.

ABOUT THE
AUTHORS

Duchess Harris, JD, PhD

Dr. Harris is a professor of American Studies at Macalester College and curator of the Duchess Harris Collection of ABDO books. She is also the coauthor of the titles in the collection, which features popular selections such as *Hidden Human Computers: The Black Women of NASA* and series including News Literacy and Being Female in America.

Before working with ABDO, Dr. Harris authored several other books on the topics of race, culture, and American history. She served as an associate editor for *Litigation News*, the American Bar Association Section of Litigation's quarterly flagship publication, and was the first editor in chief of *Law Raza*, an interactive online journal covering race and the law, published at William Mitchell College of Law. She has earned a PhD in American Studies from the University of Minnesota and a JD from William Mitchell College of Law.

Tammy Gagne

Tammy Gagne has written dozens of books for both adults and children. Her recent titles include *Carol Moseley Braun* and *Aretha Franklin*. She lives in northern New England with her husband, son, and a menagerie of pets.

INDEX